Walk!
Glenwood Springs Town and Hills

Amity Ludders

Copyright © 2013 Amity Ludders

All rights reserved.

ISBN-13: 978-1484839331

Warning:

Walking in the wilds (or in town) can be a dangerous activity carrying a risk of personal injury or death. Walking, especially in the mountains, should only be undertaken by those with a full understanding of the risks and with the training or experience to evaluate them. While every effort has been made to provide sound information within this guide, conditions can change dramatically and therefore affect the seriousness of a walk.

Therefore, the author does not accept any liability for damage of any kind (damage to property, personal injury or death) arising from use of the information in this book.

Readers are invited to contact the author with any changes relevant to the routes described within this book.

Dedicated to:

My enthusiastic walking partner,
Colleen Rutledge,
whose curiosity about our jaunts inspired me write them down.

And

Runaway,

who makes sure we get out almost every day.

Topographical Map
Glenwood Springs

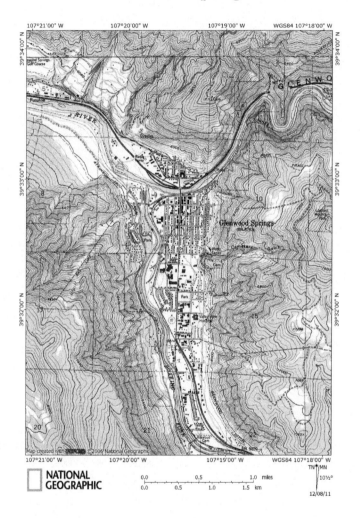

Table of Contents

Introduction	1
Maps and Navigation	5
In Town	7
Walk #1: Two Rivers Park	8
Walk #2: Downtown to 27th Street	10
Walk #3: Cardiff Glen	12
Walk #4: West Glenwood	14
Red Mountain (West)	16
Walk #5: Jeanne Golay Trail	17
Walk #6: Wulfsohn Trail and Open Space	20
Lookout Mountain (East)	22
Walk #7: Doc Holliday's	23
Walk #8: Scout Trail	26
Walk #9: Lookout Mountain Proper	30
Walk #10: Bear Creek	32
Walk #11: Red Canyon	35
Transfer Trail (North)	37
Walk #12: Transfer Trail Loop	38
Walk #13: Windy Point	41
Walk #14: Windy Point Bypass	43
Walk #15: Mitchell Creek	45

No Name (North) — 48

    Walk #16: Jess Weaver Trail — 50

    Walk #17: No Name/Grizzly Creeks — 54

    Walk #18: Windy Point via No Name — 57

    Walk #19: East No Name — 60

    Walk #20: Flat Tops Wilderness — 63

To Carbondale (South) — 66

    Walk #22: Rio Grande Bicycle Path — 67

    Walk #23: Dry Park — 69

Appendix 1: Walks by Difficulty — 71

Reading List — 73

Acknowledgements — 75

Photos by Chapter — 76

About the Author — 77

Introduction

In 2005 I had a travelling job that sent me to Glenwood Springs for an assignment. I arrived on a very hot July day and when I saw the Hot Springs Pool packed with people my first thought was, "Who would want to be in a one-hundred degree pool on a one-hundred degree day!?!" The hills were baking, dry and scrubby and having only recently come to Colorado from the West Coast, I have to admit that I initially thought that I had arrived at something of an outpost with a very large pool.

I had the good fortune of finding accommodation downtown and discovered a small but vital town center to cater to my needs that in many ways reminded me of neighborhoods in the big cities. I could walk easily to get groceries, visit the post office and use the library. What pleased me most was that the walking wasn't just effortless, it was incredibly aesthetic. Big shade trees shelter the well-maintained sidewalks on linear streets with houses big and small, many with inviting front porches often with people sitting out on them saying hello! After work I would stroll the streets admiring the shady cool of summer evenings in Glenwood Springs.

I began to learn of nearby trails and enjoyed little excursions to Red and Lookout Mountains. I have always enjoyed a good walk, and I was wowed by the fact that I could have a nearly urban experience in town but quickly escape on foot to expanses of public land. When my travelling job informed me that it was time to move on to the next assignment I gave notice and stayed put.

Glenwood Springs is a great place to go for a walk. From the center of town one can enjoy urban walks that utilize entirely paved sidewalks and bicycle trails with frequent access to town-amenities, including public transportation when the legs get tired. However, one can also quickly venture into the surrounding hills, enjoying a more adventurous walking experience on routes which take advantage of single-track as well as four-wheel drive roads. How far one might walk and what one might see is determined by constraints of time and energy, as there are routes that offer everything from a quick lunch time stroll to the lengthy all-day walkabout.

My hope is that this guide provides the walker of any ability suggestions for a great walking experience in Glenwood. Ultimately, I would like the willing walker to enjoy a taste of what I discovered here and what kept me here for seven years. With that in mind I have tried to create a comprehensive review of all of the trails, both short and long, that originate in Glenwood.

There are popular and worthy trails close by, but I've chosen to focus on walks that can be accomplished by foot from downtown Glenwood. This is partly a personal choice. I lived the car-free life in downtown and so all of my walks originated around 8th Street and Grand Avenue. I also like using downtown as the beginning and end because, in the tradition of British pub walking, I think it is fun to begin and/or end with the option of enjoying refreshment found in the cafes or restaurants that cater to all tastes and budgets. For me, there is also something fundamentally charming about the fact that visitors who arrive to Glenwood by train or bus can enjoy the town and surrounding environs entirely on foot, safely and completely car-free.

The walks are grouped into six categories based on Glenwood's geography which is very much like a compass rose. In the center are the In Town walks. To the west is Red Mountain, to the east Lookout Mountain. North of Glenwood are two distinct access points to the Flat Tops: Transfer Trail and No Name. To fit this scheme I have listed the town of Carbondale as being to the south although it is really southeast.

Walk! Glenwood Springs Town and Hills

For each walk I have provided distance and elevation information, seasonal notes, a brief description of the trail including what I think makes the walk worthwhile or noteworthy, highlights along the route, and any amenities. If there is something particularly to be aware of I have written a caveat. Please do pay attention to and heed these warnings. Detailed directions for the walk follow including directions for those using a car.

Distances have been rounded up to the nearest half or whole mile. If a route feels shorter than what is listed it is probably because it is! The distance listed is for the entire walk, from beginning to end. Most of the walks are loops so the distance is for the entire circle. Some walks have alternate routes that shorten or lengthen the walk, in these cases I have written the distance as a range from the shortest permutation to the longest. When that is the case, check in the main body of the route description for more information. If the distance has a plus sign (+) it is because there is an option for additional walking of your own choosing. Again, read the route description for more information.

My preference is to walk circles (loops) instead of lines (out-and-back on one trail), so most of the routes follow one path out and another back. If the loop is too large for one's taste then by all means walk as far as you want and turn around! I mention spots that I think make good turnarounds. Some of these loops work best walked in one direction over the other and I have generally described the loops as I best like to walk them. If they work well in either direction I try to mention it.

Each walk also has a difficulty rating. I have made my best guess based on the length of the walk, the walking surfaces and the amount of elevation gain. These ratings are fairly subjective. Appendix 1 lists the walks in order of difficulty and provides a brief explanation of why each walk got its rating to help you decide if it the walk might be a good fit for you. Not all walks are suitable for all walkers.

I have not provided estimated times with any of these walks. It is best if you have an idea of roughly how many miles per hour you walk and make your own best guess as to how long it might take you, factoring in elevation gain and weather. For the longer walks that take you away from town, plan accordingly with extra clothing, food and water.

To excuse myself from any liability I must remind readers that walking can be dangerous and that you are completely responsible for your own well-being. Trails change with time: trees fall down, rocks slide, high water washes paths away. Bad weather can turn an otherwise perfect trail into a dangerous ice chute or a mud slide. Use common sense when deciding whether to keep on or turn around.

We are lucky to have wildlife in and around Glenwood. Seeing wildlife in its own habitat is great for indulging the naturalist in all of us but it also means that the larger animals, such as bear and mountain lion, and even coyote, can present a risk. Be alert and aware when walking, especially when out in the hills. My best advice for avoiding unpleasant animal encounters is to follow a policy of "no surprises." If you notice fresh tracks or scat, hear loud rustling nearby, or even just have a funny feeling, start to sing or clap. Do not wait until it is too late and you are face to face with an unhappy animal. By letting critters know that you are coming you are being polite and safe and giving them the option of removing themselves from the immediate vicinity without the risk of confrontation. In the interest of being tuned into the environment I do not recommend the use of headphones or other auditory distractions when out on trails away from town. Please be careful! Enjoy!

Maps and Navigation

Maps

To make the most of the written descriptions in this guidebook I suggest picking up the really terrific *Glenwood Springs Trail and City Map* published by Glenwood Springs Chamber Resort Association. This map can be found for free at hotels, tourist kiosks and visitor centers. It is quite up-to-date and the city map shows everything a person needs to navigate easily all of the In Town routes.

The trail portion of the *Glenwood Springs Trail and City Map* is quite generalized and has some errors (for example, it shows that the Forest Hollow Trail intersects with Lookout Mountain Road which is not the case) but it does show the trails and roads used on these walks and in conjunction with the written descriptions in this guide would likely be adequate.

For walks that include stretches on the Rio Grande Trail, I recommend picking up the free *Rio Grande Trail Map* published by the Roaring Fork Transportation Authority. It is also available at tourist kiosks and visitor centers. This map shows the Rio Grande in its entirety, complete with locations of bathrooms, picnic tables, garbage cans and bus and automobile access.

For walks where navigation might be an issue (all routes that are rated as Expert and some rated Difficult) I would recommend carrying either USGS quads or National Geographic Trails Illustrated Maps, knowing how to read them and bringing a compass and the knowledge to use it.

The USGS topographical maps for this area have not been updated in some time. As a result some of the trails and roads which are crystal clear on the ground do not appear on the maps. Therefore use these maps as a reference, not the final word. The five quads required to cover all of the walks in this guide would be: Glenwood Springs, Carbonate, Shoshone, Cattle Creek and Carbondale. The two National Geographic Trails Illustrated Maps that cover the area are: #123 Glenwood Springs and #143 Carbondale. These maps can be purchased at any outdoor store.

A Note on GPS

I have not included GPS coordinates for any of the routes. From my personal experience I think that over-reliance on GPS can lead the walker astray faster than using one's own brain. For walks in town, for example, if one cannot find the intersection of two well-marked streets without GPS then one should probably not be out on these walks in the first place.

The great majority of the routes in this book are on clearly marked trails and roads and I would rather the walker pay attention to the scenery, the route and changing weather conditions than follow with the GPS unit in hand to the next waypoint.

If you are a GPS addict, by all means please take your GPS unit, follow the routes as described and mark waypoints for your own personal reference or post them to the internet to share with other GPS aficionados out there.

In Town

The city of Glenwood has created a striking network of paved paths that link neighborhoods to the town center. Bicycle trail, streets with sidewalks and frequent crosswalks, pedestrian-only crossings of the Colorado River and of the interstate are some of the basic features that make Glenwood so walkable. There are plenty of walks that one can take through the neighborhoods with any number of variations. The four walks here are my favorites and provide a healthy backbone for your own explorations through Glenwood's residential and commercial areas.

These walks are great all year around. The city does a fantastic job of getting out with the snowplows early, keeping routes open in all but the worst snowstorms. Nevertheless, in icy conditions be mindful of slick spots.

Well-maintained paved surfaces, fun public art, attractive landscaping and encounters with friendly locals are some of the things I look forward to when I set out for a walk around Glenwood.

Walk #1: Two Rivers Park

Downtown to Two Rivers Park, past the Hot Springs Pool and back to town.

Distance: 1.5 miles

Elevation Gain: 70 feet

Difficulty: Easy

Seasons: All year

Description: This short loop is an easy leg-stretcher, get-the-blood-flowing kind of walk. Perfect for lunch time or a quick loop after work with the dog and kids. Fine walking in any weather.

Highlights: The junction of the Roaring Fork and Colorado Rivers, two great pedestrian/bicycle only bridges, Firefighters Memorial in Two Rivers Park.

Amenities: Water and bathrooms at the park.

Directions: From 8th Street and the west side of Grand Avenue in downtown Glenwood, follow the pedestrian mall down to 7th Street. Turn left on 7th and continue on the sidewalk, which is on the south side of the street. Just after passing under an old Rio Grande railroad span over the road painted with murals of horses, notice a funeral home on the north side of the street (on the right). Cross the street here at a crosswalk and follow a spur path onto the Rio Grande Trail. Turn right (north) onto the paved bicycle path and continue along, crossing a substantial bridge across the Colorado. Make an immediate left to loop around the park, stopping at the Firefighters Memorial at the west end of the park before circling the ball fields and returning to the bridge. Instead of crossing back over the bridge, continue straight ahead paralleling the Colorado on its north side to a lighted crossing of the east-bound entrance to I-70. Continue underneath the interstate and after crossing the off-ramp of I-70 turn right

Walk! Glenwood Springs Town and Hills

on N. River Street toward the Hot Springs Pool (signed). Walk through the ample parking lot to stairs which lead up to paved path looping under the Grand Avenue bridge. The pool comes into sight. Turn right (south) onto the pedestrian bridge, arriving back at 7th and Grand.

With a car: Drive to Two Rivers Park for plenty of parking and begin the loop from there.

Walk #2: Downtown to 27th Street

Downtown to 27th Street via sidewalks on Midland, return to town on the Rio Grande Trail.

Distance: 4.0 miles

Elevation Gain: 120 feet

Difficulty: Easy

Seasons: All year

Caveat: During snowy, icy days before sidewalks have been shoveled, the walk along Midland can be treacherous.

Description: A pleasant walk through Veltus Park, past residences and onto the Rio Grande Trail. Like Walk #1, this is a good option for lunchtime or after work as commitment of time or energy is not particularly great.

Highlights: Veltus Park and old jail, open spaces along the Roaring Fork behind the High School (watch for paragliders!)

Amenities: No water or bathrooms on route, but Rio Grande passes behind stores and businesses located on Grand Avenue.

Directions: From 8th Street and the west side of Grand Avenue in downtown Glenwood, follow the pedestrian mall down to 7th Street. Turn left on 7th and stay on the sidewalk (left side of the street). Immediately after crossing the Roaring Fork River and noticing some attractive public art painted on an electrical box and trash can, turn left onto a paved path heading into Veltus Park. Follow the path through the park to the automobile entrance on Midland Avenue. Turn left (south) onto sidewalk and continue along Midland until 27th street. At 27th Street consider continuing to Cardiff Glen as described in Walk #3.

Otherwise, turn left at 27th, cross the Roaring Fork River and turn left (north). Continue on S. Grand Avenue past the Rivers Restaurant and other businesses to the Rio Grande Trail. Stay on the Rio Grande, passing behind the high school and elementary school, until crossing underneath 7th Street. Look for a spur path on the right to reach 7th. Cross to the south side of the street and follow sidewalk into town. Alternately, from the Rio Grande path, cut up 12th Street into neighborhoods and follow Pitkin, Colorado or Grand north until back at 8th Street.

With a car: Park at Veltus Park or behind the High School.

Walk #3: Cardiff Glen

Twenty-Seventh Street to historic Cardiff Glen via Atkinson Trail, circling Airport to coke ovens and back to the Atkinson.

Distance: 4.0 – 8.0 miles

Elevation Gain: 300 feet

Difficulty: Easy

Seasons: All year

Description: This is a delightful walk with plenty of variety. The walk begins along the beautiful Atkinson trail paralleling the Roaring Fork River, continues into the residential neighborhood of Cardiff Glen, follows paved path high above the river passing the old Cardiff school house en route to the airport which marks the southern end of the route. From the airport swing north past coke ovens, stopping to read the informational plaque, into the tiny commercial center of Cardiff Glen. Just north of the gas station and market return to the Atkinson trail.

Highlights: Atkinson Trail, old Cardiff school house, Glenwood airport, historic coke ovens.

Amenities: Water and bathrooms near ball field on route in Cardiff Glen. Small market and gas station in Cardiff.

Directions: To arrive at 27th street from downtown, follow directions for Walk #2 in either direction (Rio Grande or along Midland) or take the Ride Glenwood bus from 9th and Grand to its stop on 27th Street. Beginning from downtown, the entire loop is 8.0 miles.

At 27th Street, at the northwest corner of the bridge crossing the Roaring Fork River follow clear path onto the Atkinson trail which parallels the river on its western bank. Follow the paved path as it reaches a riverside picnic area and then makes a distinct ninety degree turn away from the river. In short order a lesser path branches left across a small bridge. Follow this path. Arriving in a residential neighborhood alongside a pocket park, jog briefly left and then continue straight ahead (south) on sidewalked Mountain Drive until reaching Mt. Sopris Drive, noticing Mt. Sopris Elementary School and ball fields ahead. Turn left, continuing into the neighborhood. When the road you have been following ends, turning into a T, go right into the cul-de-sac. On your left you will spot a paved bicycle/pedestrian path, the Park East Nature Trail. Follow this path well above the river, past the old Cardiff school house and river fishing access until it arrives once again on a neighborhood street, Sky Ranch Drive. Turn left and continue as it turns into Airport Road (no sidewalk but almost no traffic either) passing the airport runway (which will be on the right). Follow the road as it loops around the end of the airport and bends back toward Cardiff. After approximately ¼ mile notice the coke ovens in the hillside on your left. Continue along passing a variety of buildings to the gas station and market. Immediately north of the market, pick up the Atkinson Trail again by following the paved path east, to the river and then north, back to 27th Street.

With a car: Park in Cardiff Glen at river access trailhead and parking area next to the gas station and market.

Walk #4: West Glenwood

Downtown to West Glenwood via Donegan Road. Up Mitchell Creek Road to the Fish Hatchery, returning to town along the Colorado River on Devereux Road and through Two Rivers Park.

Distance: 8.5 miles

Elevation Gain: 700 feet

Difficulty: Moderate

Seasons: All year

Description: This walk makes a sizable loop passing a number of Glenwood landmarks and provides good contrast between the bustle of Highway 6 & 24, safely noted from a bicycle/pedestrian path, to the pastoral setting of the fish hatchery. The walk back along Devereux Road and the Colorado River is pleasant.

Highlights: Hot Springs Pool, Hotel Colorado, Colorado State Fish Hatchery, Whitewater Park, Firefighters Memorial, Two Rivers Park.

Amenities: Water and bathrooms at fish hatchery visitor building and Two Rivers Park. Convenience stores and Mall at I-70 interchange.

Directions: From 8th Street and the west side of Grand Avenue in downtown Glenwood follow the pedestrian mall to 7th Street. Cross 7th to stairs (ahead and slightly to the right) leading up to the pedestrian-only bridge across the Colorado River. Continue to 6th street and cross to the corner with the Hotel Colorado. At this point there is a choice: either turn left (west) on 6th and follow this busy road on sidewalks and then bicycle path until Donegan Road; alternatively, take the more peaceful neighborhood route by continuing north, uphill, and then left (west) on 5th until Laurel Street. Follow Laurel north to where it turns into Linden Street. Continue on Linden until it intersects with Hwy 6 & 24. From here all paths come together. Follow Hwy. 6 until encountering Donegan Road veering off on the right. Stay on Donegan as it travels west through residential areas until it ends at Mitchell Creek Road. Turn right and follow the ascending road to the Colorado State Fish Hatchery. Enjoy feeding the trout in their runs (fish food vending machine on electrical pole next to fish runs) and check out the tiny visitor's center.

The Fish Hatchery marks the turnaround. Head back down Mitchell Creek Road, turning left (east) onto Donegan Road. Proceed along Donegan until Mel-Ray Road. Turn right (south), walking toward Hwy. 6 & 24 and I-70. From this lively intersection one can catch the Ride Glenwood bus back into town, if need be.

Proceed on foot and carefully cross Hwy. 6 & 24 using the crosswalk on the east side of the roundabout, heading under I-70. The Colorado River and Whitewater Park come into view on the left. Cross the bridge, enjoying the show of kayakers battling the waves. Take an immediate left onto Devereux Road. Follow Devereux as it parallels the Colorado eventually crossing the river on a bridge to Two Rivers Park (the sidewalk will end a little before the river crossing and the park, but the shoulder is ample and traffic is usually light and polite).

From Two Rivers Park, follow paths toward town. See Walk #1 for details.

With a car: Park at Two Rivers Park, the Glenwood Mall or at the Fish Hatchery.

Red Mountain (West)

Red Mountain is the aptly named mountain to the immediate west of downtown Glenwood. I have also heard Red Mountain referred to as the "hill with the cross" as it has an illuminated cross during the holidays of Christmas and Easter. A maintained road switchbacks up to the top and provides a relatively easy way to gain elevation and excellent views of Glenwood, the Roaring Fork Valley and the Elk Range. The overlook is 1700 feet above Glenwood. A network of single-track trails, much steeper and a little more rugged than the road, also laces its way up to the viewpoint. Alternating between trail and the road makes for a fun and varied walk. Because of its east-facing aspect, Red Mountain catches the earliest morning light. On hot days, go early or late in the day. Paragliders are often seen near the viewpoint taking advantage of morning thermals.

Walk #5: Jeanne Golay Trail

Downtown to Red Mountain trailhead, up road or on single-track to viewpoint.

Distance: 4.0 – 7.0 miles

Elevation Gain: 1700 feet

Difficulty: Moderate

Seasons: All year

Caveats: During mud season and icy winter days both the road and trail can be frightfully slippery and are best left alone. In summer, this trail can become quite hot and sunburnt mid-day. Also, bears and mountain lions frequent Red Mountain. Be alert.

Description: This walk is a local favorite and for good reason. The combination of road and trail walking keeps it interesting for the legs and the ever-expanding views keep calling one onward and upward.

Highlights: Several outstanding overlooks from which to survey the area.

Amenities: Two well-placed benches: the first is approximately one-quarter of the way up, the second is at the three-quarter mark. No water or bathrooms.

Note on Distance: Because of the myriad options for getting to the top, the total mileage varies fairly significantly. Walking roundtrip from downtown and staying entirely on the road is about 7.0 miles. Following the trail whenever possible brings the mileage down to 5.0 miles from town. Parking at the trailhead takes approximately one mile off the entire walk, whether road or trail is taken. In spite of the difference in mileage, one's walking time may not be impacted at all as the shorter route is also considerably steeper.

Directions: From 8th Street and the west side of Grand Avenue in downtown Glenwood follow the pedestrian mall to 7th Street. Turn left (west) on 7th and stay on the sidewalk (left side of the street) until the lighted intersection at Midland Avenue. Cross at the light and continue straight ahead following a short, well-landscaped, switch-backing city path up the bank. Turn left on Red Mountain Drive for a few feet and then right on W. 9th Street, ascending briefly to the well-marked Red Mountain Trailhead sporting an informational sign worth reading.

From here the choices begin: Stay on the paved road which will turn to natural surfaces just beyond the water treatment plant and follow it all the way to the top (the road will level out and you will see the cross and a few other installations when you have reached the end). Steps before the cross, notice a well-used path on the left (east). Leave the road and follow this path to a lovely red rock from which to survey the landscape, views unobstructed by the scrub oak.

Or, from the trailhead pick up the wide gravelly trail (passing a very attractive, newer information sign) and continue to a crossing of the road. Look across the road (at about 11 o'clock) to notice a carsonite post marking a well-used path through the grass. Follow this to a three-way fork at the bottom of the hill: one path continues straight up on rocky tread, while another bends off to the left and slightly behind. These are both good choices. If the hill suddenly seems too steep for one's taste, the third track, on the far right, leads to the fenced off water tank and the paved road. Assuming that one opts for the trails instead of bailing for the road, both routes will intersect with the road a little ways up, near the first bench. Continue looking for trail, which tends to follow the ridge and is signed with carsonite posts in places. Sometimes the trail is quite steep and adheres to the most direct route possible. Other times, it makes pleasant rambling

Walk! Glenwood Springs Town and Hills

switchbacks. Where there isn't obvious trail, stay on the road keeping eyes open for the next bit of trail. The trail is not continuous so have fun piecing together a route of your liking.

Getting lost would be hard. As long as you continue working your way upward on road or trail (not through the brush!) you cannot go wrong.

After the viewpoint the road does continue, pleasantly flat and contouring, with more fine views until encountering clearly marked private property. Any distance beyond the cross is purely extra credit.

Pick a route down, road or trail, back to the trailhead.

With a car: Park at the Red Mountain Trailhead.

Walk #6: Wulfsohn Trail and Open Space

Downtown to Red Mountain trailhead, then along contouring path to the Wulfsohn Open Space and Road.

Distance: 3.0+ miles

Elevation Gain: 240 feet

Difficulty: Easy

Seasons: All year

Caveats: Keep an eye out for wildlife. Bears, mountain lions and coyotes are all active in this area.

Description: This is a fun little connector trail that goes from the Red Mountain Trailhead to the Wulfsohn Open Space behind the Meadows Shopping Center. This path provides a nice traffic-free alternative to the bicycle path that parallels Midland. There are plenty of options upon arriving at the Open Space. Explore the paths of the open space, take care of shopping errands, visit the Community Recreation Center or just turn around back to town. From downtown to Wulfsohn Road is 1.5 miles.

Highlights: Community Recreation Center, Community Garden, Wulfsohn Open Space.

Amenities: Water and bathrooms at the Recreation Center and at the shopping center.

Directions: Follow directions for Walk #5 to the Red Mountain Trailhead. Once at the trailhead, follow the gravel trail (not the road) past a garbage can and an information kiosk. Within steps, look for two sapling size trees and a level trail between them heading right (west). Follow this path as it smoothly contours around the base of the hill, staying above Midland Avenue. Stay on the trail as Wulfsohn Road, the Community Recreation Center, Community Garden and the Meadows Shopping Center all come into view. Follow trails and gravel road to paved Wulfsohn Road and the shopping center or stay on the trail you are on to wind through the open space. The choices are many and it is all up to you! It is 1.5 miles from downtown to Wulfsohn Road at the Meadows. Add miles with a walk on trails through the open space.

The trails through the open space are clear and often signed. With the shopping center in view almost continuously it would be challenging to get lost. Most of the trails follow an east-west orientation, with three access points down to Wulfsohn Road. The first access point (east end of Wulfsohn Road near the hotels and Community Recreation Center) is at Wulfsohn Road and E. Meadows Drive. The second access point is west of the shopping center, just off of Wulfsohn Road at the City of Glenwood Springs Operations Facility. At the very western end of Wulfsohn Road, the Wulfsohn trail intersects with the road.

After exploring the open space or shopping center, return to Wulfsohn Road and E. Meadows Drive to return to the Red Mountain trailhead. Alternately, on the north side of the Community Recreation Center, pick up the bicycle path and follow it back to 7th and downtown Glenwood.

With a car: Park at Red Mountain Trailhead, the Community Recreation Center or the Meadows Shopping Center.

Lookout Mountain (East)

Lookout Mountain frames Glenwood to the east, sitting opposite Red Mountain. These two mountains together, one on either side of the junction of the Roaring Fork and Colorado rivers, form the gateway to the Roaring Fork Valley. Of the two mountains, Lookout is the wilder and offers many more miles of walking for the simple fact that the land is more public than private. There are three popular trails that get most of the use on Lookout and create several great loop walks. However, by expanding out onto jeep road one can create even larger loops, including a complete circumambulation of Lookout Mountain. For this reason Lookout Mountain is popular with mountain bikers as well. Facing west, Lookout enjoys long afternoon sunlight. In the summer this can make for hot walking; however, in spring and fall when days are cooler and shorter or even on a summer evening, catching the last afternoon light from Lookout can be sheer delight. On summer afternoons paragliders launch from Lookout.

During snowy winters the first mile on each of the trails usually gets enough traffic that the snow is well-packed and walkable. Beyond that, snowshoes are de rigueur. If planning a snowshoe trip give yourself plenty of time. For this reason I have listed these as three-season trails. In my estimation these routes do not get enough traffic to make them viable winter options, unless it is a very low snow year. As for snowshoeing expeditions for those not faint of heart, Lookout has a lot to offer!

The trails that traverse Lookout can all be worked into loops that build on one another in length and elevation. Therefore, there is a lot of flexibility in setting out on a walk on Lookout. If one is half-way up the mountain and wants more, there are options to keep going. The walks in this section are listed in order of increasing length.

Walk #7: Doc Holliday's

Downtown to the 12th Street cut and the Linwood Pioneer Cemetery to Forest Hollow trail and back to town on the Scout Trail.

Distance: 6.0 miles

Elevation Gain: 1800 feet

Difficulty: Moderate

Seasons: All but winter, unless carrying snowshoes.

Caveats: In the winter or mud season, the road to the cemetery can be extremely slick. Beyond the cemetery keep an eye out for bears and mountain lions.

Description: A favorite for locals and tourists alike. The walk to and around the cemetery makes a fine outing in and of itself without continuing one step beyond. The cemetery has attractive informational signs that should not be missed. Beyond the cemetery, single-track trail parallels Cemetery Gulch and then carries the walker up a couple of switchbacks, crosses the arm of a ridge with good views of Glenwood, continues on old jeep track contouring and climbing slightly to a beautiful sage-brush meadow with outstanding views south. From the meadow, continue left along jeep track past an old corral to where the narrowing track begins to contour along the side of Lookout Mountain. Arrive at a junction with the unsigned Scout Trail on the left (west) which leads back to 8th Street and downtown.

Highlights: Linwood Pioneer Cemetery, sage meadow viewpoint of Mt. Sopris, Scout Trail

Amenities: Water at the Linwood Pioneer Cemetery trailhead.

Directions: From 8th Street and Grand Avenue in downtown Glenwood head east on 8th street three blocks to Bennett Avenue. Take a right on Bennett and continue a short distance past 11th street to the well-marked Pioneer Cemetery trailhead on the left (east) side of the street. If you find yourself at 13th street, you've gone too far. Tank up on water here as there isn't any farther along. Follow the trail as it winds up and around the west-facing hill to the cemetery. Follow signs to Doc Holliday's grave, noticing other unique gravestones as you go. At this point you are a little over one mile from downtown and at a good place to turn around or keep going.

To continue on, briefly walk through the cemetery on the main trail to the northeast corner and a fence that marks the cemetery boundary. In the fence is an exit through which you go, bringing you to an old jeep trail and a yellow gate. Pass around the gate on obvious trail and continue up on this path (grown over jeep trail). After paralleling Cemetery Gulch, which will be well below and on the left (north) for a distance, the trail will fork. The right fork follows a moderate, switch-backing course while the left fork takes a steeper, more direct route. All paths eventually come together on the edge of a ridge arm with views of Glenwood. The jeep trail/single-track route now levels out for a short distance before climbing through sage and scrub oak to an open sagebrush meadow with outstanding views of the Elk Range.

From here, turn left (east) onto more overgrown but well-walked 4WD track, soon passing the remains of an old corral (on the right). Stay on this path (Forest Hollow Trail) for approximately 1.5 miles as it continues swinging around to the north, contouring along the flanks of Lookout Mountain. Your next trail is the Scout Trail which will be a prominent, well-used trail on your left. The junction of the Forest Hollow and Scout Trails is not signed although there is a carsonite post with the word "Trail" on it. Turn left and begin a steady descent. The trail is clear and easy to follow as it swings down onto a ridge, with excellent views of Horseshoe Bend on the Colorado River, and then continues steadily descending along exposed, west-facing slopes toward town. The trail pops out at the end of 8th Street. Continue down 8th Street back to Grand Avenue.

Also, this loop works well in either direction. To avoid the mental gymnastics of reversing the route, look to Walk #8 to get started up Scout Trail.

With a car: Look for street parking near the Pioneer Cemetery.

Walk #8: Scout Trail

Downtown to Scout Trail trailhead to the top of Lookout Mountain at the radio towers, back down following telephone poles to the Doc Holliday trail, Pioneer Cemetery and into town.

Distance: 6.0 miles

Elevation Gain: 2300 feet

Difficulty: Moderate

Seasons: All but winter

Caveats: Mountain bikers use Scout Trail and sometimes descend quite quickly. Keep an eye out for wildlife.

Description: The Scout Trail is another local favorite and a great way to get to the top of Lookout Mountain. The trail provides a consistently graded, steadily ascending route to the top. The views along the trail are excellent, first of Glenwood and then the Glenwood Canyon and the Colorado River and finally of Mt. Sopris and the Elk Range. Once at the top of Lookout there is no reason not to turn around and follow the Scout Trail back to town. It is not necessary to make a loop. However, there is a nice alternative route so I have provided the directions. If one goes up and down on Scout Trail I would rate the difficulty as moderate. Taking the alternate definitely kicks the rating up to Difficult. Additionally, there is a more direct route than Scout Trail to the top of Lookout. I provide the details at the end of this walk.

Highlights: Scout Trail with views of Glenwood, Glenwood Canyon, Mt. Sopris.

Amenities: Water at Pioneer Cemetery trailhead (if one makes the loop and ends at cemetery).

Directions: From 8th Street and Grand Avenue in downtown Glenwood follow 8th east to its end at the base of Lookout Mountain. The trailhead may not be immediately obvious. It is at the end of a driveway on the left (north). An informational sign marks the spot.

Within a few steps of beginning, the walker is greeted with a choice of three trails. These trails quickly come together again so proceed up either the left or right fork. The middle trail should not be used due to erosion. At the top of this initial steep rise all trails join into one well-used path soon passing a log bench alongside the trail before settling into an easier grade. The trail winds in and out of drainages as it works its way up the dry western facing slopes of Lookout Mountain.

Continue on the trail, upwards, to a clear junction with the Forest Hollow Trail (unsigned). Turn left for a few level steps and then take a right onto the continuation of the Scout Trail. If the trail seems too flat for too long, you have most likely gone too far and are probably enjoying the Forest Hollow Trail. The Scout Trail continues upward, switch-backing to the top of Lookout Mountain. The trail ends unceremoniously at the edge of a gravel jeep road, Lookout Mountain Road, in a grove of scrub oak. A few concrete picnic tables and fire pits are in the shrubbery nearby. Turn left (north) on the road for a few more upward steps and a fine viewpoint of the area. A radio installation looms behind.

From here, turn around and head back down the Scout Trail or consider taking the following alternate route, which is more challenging.

Where the Scout Trail meets the road, turn right (south) and walk a short distance to the first, lesser used grassy road that one encounters on the right, heading west. Turn onto this road for a few paces. Notice the telephone poles also descending from the hill. The telephone poles will be your guide. Where the road bends to the north, notice a row of red boulders ahead, to the west, in the grass. Here, leave the road for the telephone pole cut. Walk over the row of red boulders toward the first telephone pole, and at the crest of the hill see a line of poles marching down the hill. If you cannot pick out a distinct trail yet, that is okay. This is your route. The telephone pole cut is rockier and less-used than the Scout Trail, although faint tread should become discernible.

As you are descending notice the clear 4WD track, now well below, ahead and to the right. This is the path that comes out of the Pioneer Cemetery (see Walk #7) and this is what you are aiming for. Notice the telephone poles below and how they make a definite turn south following a minor drainage. Continue downhill to the point where the route just begins to completely level out, just before the telephone line heads south. Half way between the last two poles (before they make the turn) in the middle of this level stretch with exuberant sage brush, a faint trail branches to the right (northwest) between sage brush and scrub oak, climbing gently over a little ridge and immediately meeting with the 4WD track that you noticed from above.

Take a left onto this clear track, which is actually the Forest Hollow Trail (it you turn right you will return to the Scout Trail). You will soon notice a definite fork in the path. Stay to the right (west) and follow this trail past the remains of an old corral (on the left, to the south) to a four way intersection in a sage brush meadow. Turn right (north) and follow the path as it descends onto a contouring old jeep road. Continue to a ridge-top fork and choose between either moderate switchbacks (the left, west fork) or the more direct route heading north/northwest. All routes come together. On clear trail, parallel Cemetery Gulch to the northern edge of the cemetery (fence with opening marks the spot). Walk through the cemetery and down to the trailhead. Or, stay on the road past the northern perimeter of the cemetery as it descends also toward the trailhead. At 12th and Bennett Avenue follow streets of your choice through the neighborhood back to 8th and Grand.

Note: This loop works well in either direction. To start at the Cemetery, follow Walk #7 to the old corral and onto the Forest Hollow trail noticing the line of telephone poles on the hillside. Just as the road begins to bend north, look for a path on the right (south) through the sage brush. This little connector will take you over the ridge and down to the telephone poles which you will follow up to the top of Lookout at the radio towers.

With a car: Look for street parking on 8th Street.

Variation: For those training for Mt. Everest there is an alternate route to the top of Lookout Mountain that is considerably shorter and steeper than the Scout Trail. This variation gets considerably less use and the surface deserves a little more caution. I mention it only for those who are feeling intrepid and up for a little lung-busting. From the Scout Trail trailhead proceed along the trail to the log bench on the right at the top of the first rise. Face the bench. Immediately right of the bench is a wash with loose rock. Up you go! The hideous start quickly turns into a more trail-like surface. Stay on this trail all the way to the top or when this direct route crosses first the Forest Hollow Trail and then the Scout Trail (crossing it three times) jump off for a more mellow walk.

Walk #9: Lookout Mountain Proper

Scout Trail to Forest Hollow Trail to Lookout Mountain Trail. Turnaround back to town.

Distance: 12.0 miles

Elevation Gain: 3000 feet

Difficulty: Difficult

Seasons: All but winter, unless carrying snowshoes.

Caveats: Really watch for wildlife on the trail up to the top of Lookout Mountain. This trail doesn't get a lot of traffic and is great habitat for animals large and small. In spring, snow can linger on north-facing Forest Hollow Trail making the trail largely impassable.

Description: Lookout Mountain is known to most by the radio towers that can be seen from downtown Glenwood. However, the actual top of Lookout Mountain is two miles farther east. This is a long walk that provides plenty of time to be awe-struck by the Colorado River as it carves its way through the Glenwood Canyon. The top of Lookout Mountain proper is forested so lacks stellar views but the walk up can be quite pleasing. Glimpses of the Canyon through the trees are stunning. In the summer, wildflowers in the understory are bright and colorful.

Highlights: Scout Trail, Forest Hollow Trail, canyon views.

Amenities: None.

Directions: Follow Walk #8 to its junction with the Forest Hollow Trail. Take a left onto Forest Hollow and continue on this pleasantly level, contouring path as it winds in and out of forest high above the Colorado River for a little over two miles to a signed junction with the Lookout Mountain Trail.

Turn right (south) and follow the trail as it gradually climbs and then begins to switchback to the top of Lookout Mountain. From the top (because it is forested and Lookout does not have a prominent top, there is a certain anti-climax to making it this far) one may notice Lookout Mountain Road a very short distance below. Alas! The land between you and the road is private property! Time to turn around and head back the way you came.

If one could drop down to Lookout Mountain Road, one would take a right (north) and follow the road back to the radio towers above Glenwood. From the radio towers, one could descend to town by the Scout Trail or the telephone pole alternative as described in Walk #8.

With a car: Look for street parking on 8th Street.

Walk #10: Bear Creek

Downtown to Lookout Mountain at the radio towers, along Lookout Mountain Road to a 4WD track into Bear Creek. Forest Hollow Trail to Scout Trail and back to town.

Distance: 14.5 miles

Elevation Gain: 3300 feet

Difficulty: Difficult

Seasons: All but winter, unless carrying snowshoes

Caveats: Watch for wildlife

Description: A good long walk on great trail with attractive scenery. The walk begins along the Scout Trail to the top of Lookout Mountain at the radio towers. From here, one follows Lookout Mountain Road to the end of its first switchback where one jumps off onto lesser used 4WD track for a pleasantly rolling walk through cattle land. The road drops into a cool, forested hollow from which one departs the road for trail which continues into the Bear Creek drainage. The signed Forest Hollow Trail has its eastern terminus here. From here it is a largely flat but long walk back to the Scout Trail and town.

Highlights: Scout Trail, Bear Creek, Forest Hollow Trail, territorial views.

Amenities: Bear Creek often has water but it can also have a lot of cows. Bring a water filter.

Directions: Follow Walk #8 to the top of Lookout Mountain at the radio towers and Lookout Mountain Road. At the road, turn right (south) and stay on the road as it climbs gently along the open hillside with excellent views of the valley and the Elk Range. Soon after passing an open meadow with a cattle pond on the left, the road passes a sign that reads "Leaving Public Lands". Continue on the road, passing a driveway on the right where the road makes a ninety degree turn. The road swings through a little aspen grove and around a clearing with two small ponds (on the right). Gooseberry Park Drive branches off to the left. Stay on Lookout Mountain Road as it begins a steady descent with views of Spring Valley. When the road begins to make its first switchback, look for a 4WD track on the left (south), at the end of the switchback. Follow this rudimentary track a short distance and notice a gate marked "no trespassing." The track you are on continues just to the right of this gate and to a three way junction. A carsonite post with an arrow marks the way to the left. If you were to go to the right you would come to the parking area for these ATV routes. Follow the arrow and continue on the road across a worn cattle grate. Stay on this road as it bends east and then north and drops into a hollow. The road begins to leave the drainage, drops again and just before it begins to climb very steeply, possibly signed as FS 408, notice single-track on the left returning back to the drainage.

Follow the clear, well-used single-track into the Bear Creek drainage. A little marsh of cattails on the right signals proximity to the signed Forest Hollow Trail on the left. If you have a filter and need water, follow Bear Creek on old jeep track, north, down the drainage to where the creek sounds a little more melodious for better water. Otherwise, turn onto the Forest Hollow Trail and begin the long walk back to Glenwood. Views of the Glenwood Canyon are breath-taking and ease the miles. After two miles you will notice the signed Lookout Mountain Trail (Walk #9). Unless you feel like a lot of extra credit, stay on the Forest Hollow Trail for another couple of miles to its junction with the Scout Trail. Down the Scout Trail and back to town!

Note: This loop could be walked in either direction although this way, as described, is my preference. In the afternoon Lookout Mountain Road can become quite toasty. I prefer a cool walk on Lookout Mountain Road and then a cool walk through forest on Lookout's north side.

With a car: Look for street parking on 8th.

Walk #11: Red Canyon

Downtown to Scout Trail to Lookout Mountain Road to Red Canyon Road and back to Glenwood on the Rio Grande Trail.

Distance: 15.5 miles

Elevation Gain: 3000 feet

Difficulty: Moderate

Seasons: All but winter (unless feeling adventurous and ready for snow travel)

Caveats: Red Canyon can be baking hot and dry in the height of summer. No water is available so plan hydration accordingly. Also, Red Canyon Road is narrow and winding so be mindful of approaching vehicles.

Description: This route is one of my favorites. For its length I think it is surprisingly easy as the trail and road surfaces are good and make for speedy travel. The long descent from Lookout Mountain Road to the Rio Grande also helps keep the pace strong. This route is great for trail running. Red Canyon Road is exciting as it hugs the canyon wall above a deep drainage. Look for cars below that didn't quite make the turn. Traffic is usually fairly light and going slowly but stay alert for drivers who may not be expecting foot traffic.

Highlights: Scout Trail, Lookout Mountain Road, Red Canyon Road

Amenities: The Roaring Fork Marketplace on Hwy. 82 opposite the Rio Grande Trail, two miles from downtown and the end of the walk, has all amenities.

Directions: Follow Walk #8, up Scout Trail to the top of Lookout Mountain at the radio towers. Turn south (right) on Lookout Mountain Road and follow this moderately maintained dirt road with excellent valley views as it first climbs gently yet steadily and then begins a gradual switchbacking descent to its end at paved CR 115, Red Canyon Road. Turn right (north) and continue as this road bends west and turns into a nicely surfaced dirt road. Admire the red walls of the canyon, hopefully a slice of blue sky overhead and birds flitting in the pines. After just over two miles Red Canyon Road ends at Hwy. 82.

Cross the highway very carefully and pick up the paved Rio Grande trail where it crosses the Holy Cross driveway. Turn right (north) onto the bicycle path and continue three miles to downtown Glenwood, exiting the path at either 12th Street or at 7th (see Walk #2 for details, if needed).

Note: This loop works well in either direction. My preference is for a more direct ascent and a longer more gradual descent, hence my decision to describe it as I have.

With a car: Look for street parking on 8th Street or park at the Rio Grande parking area just south of the Rosebud Cemetery on CR 154. Begin the loop from here by following the Rio Grande into town and then to the Scout Trail.

Transfer Trail (North)

Glenwood's backdrop to the north is a formidable formation reaching over 10,000 feet before leveling off to a rolling landscape of forest and parkland cut by canyon-like drainages. This area is known as the Flat Tops and if one proceeds far enough north one encounters the Flat Tops Wilderness, the second largest wilderness in Colorado. The Flat Tops is awe-inspiring for its vastness and its impressive collection of wildlife. Islands of forest surrounded by meadow provide outstanding habitat for a variety of animals. Lakes, streams, and rock formations with fossils all make the Flat Tops eye-catching and noteworthy, a place that inspires a sense of discovery.

From downtown Glenwood it is possible to wander up these slopes. In many ways, the walks up to this landscape are not so different than climbing a fourteener (Colorado mountains over 14,000 feet). Total elevation gain and distance are very comparable. In other words, one does not need to leave town to get an outstanding workout or train for bigger things!

South-facing, the Transfer Trail is sun exposed most of the day. In the heat of summer this can be a drawback, but the rest of the year it is a plus. On cool days or in the winter the sun adds warmth and the road will often stay snow free longer than other routes mentioned so far. Once the winter sets in, snowmobilers make use of Transfer Trail, keeping it packed for surprisingly easy walking with or without the snowshoes.

During summer weekends Transfer Trail is popular with ATVers. I'd recommend staying far away unless you are craving a steady diet of dust sandwiches! Also, the Flat Tops offer some of the finest elk hunting in the state. During the fall wear blaze orange and stay on roads.

Walk #12: Transfer Trail Loop

Downtown to Hwy. 6 &24, Traver Trail Road to Transfer Trail (FS 602) for a little loop and back to town.

Distance: 11.0 miles

Elevation Gain: 2900 feet

Difficulty: Moderate

Seasons: All but winter

Caveats: Watch for wildlife

Description: More familiar to motor sport enthusiasts than walkers, this route provides a great leg-stretcher for the more ambitious walker. On weekdays throughout the year it is entirely possible to have this walk to oneself and not see a soul. The route provides a fair bit of variety as one walks upwards through the different zones created by the altitude. Begin in scrub oak and pine to aspen groves. There are two possible starts to this walk at the Traver/Transfer Trail junction. The distance listed is if one takes the single-track route one way and the road the other. Using only the single-track shaves one mile off the total distance. Parking at the pull-out on Traver Trail reduces the total mileage by two miles. Parking at the saddle reduces the total distance to five miles with only 1500 feet of gain.

Highlights: Good viewpoints, elk sightings.

Amenities: None.

Directions: From 8th Street and the west side of Grand Avenue in downtown Glenwood follow the pedestrian mall to 7th Street. Cross 7th, notice stairs ahead and to your right. Follow them and continue across the Colorado River on the pedestrian only bridge, noticing the Hot Springs Pool and the Hotel Colorado. Cross to the corner with the Hotel. Continue up the street past the west entrance of the hotel to 5th Street. Turn left on 5th to Laurel Street, which turns into Linden as it bends west. Follow Linden to its end at Hwy. 6&24. Turn right (west) and follow on sidewalk past a parking area to Traver Trail, a road cutting up the hill on the right. Follow Traver Trail as it makes a ninety-degree bend to the north. Just when Traver Trail begins to make a distinct U back to the south, notice unpaved Transfer Trail taking off from the bottom of the U and an informational sign for the Transfer Trail on the north side of the road. A rough pull-out parking area is to the right of the sign.

From here there is a choice:

One can follow the road, Transfer Trail, which is fairly low traffic (although a quarry above can send a steady stream of heavily loaded trucks down the hill at times), until an obvious saddle that sits between the back side of the Glenwood Caverns (hill with the gondola on it) and the hill leading to the Flat Tops. From here there are good views into the Canyon and of West Glenwood and beyond.

Alternatively and preferably, look to the right of the sign and the northeast end of the pull-out. A rough trail begins alongside a very minor drainage. Follow this trail up onto the ridge, eventually intersecting Transfer Trail Road at the end of a switchback. As you ascend, you will notices forks in this trail. The choice is always between longer switchbacks or a direct, steeper route. Make your own decision as all paths eventually join together. Once at the road, continue upwards (right), steadily climbing to the saddle mentioned in the paragraph above.

At the saddle continue north toward the big hill in front of you and an attractive cut metal sign announces the Transfer Trail and the 4WD club. Turn right (the only way to go, really) onto rougher 4WD track and follow along enjoying the views and keeping an eye out for wildlife. After not even a mile, notice a rougher track joining the road you are on from the west. You will soon be coming down this very road. In the meanwhile continue on the road you are following as it begins to climb quite steadily and steeply alongside the right (east) side of the Cascade Creek drainage. The trail levels out for a short stretch as it comes into the drainage and then climbs a little more where it crosses the drainage in a prominent U.

Onwards and upwards, you soon come to the first really great viewpoint. On the left (south) a well-used flat area with fire rings and various detritus offers panoramic views of all lands south. Back on the road continue climbing a little farther until encountering a distinct road on your left, heading west, northwest. FS 602 continues straight ahead. Turn left onto this lesser-used road. This is the same road that you saw intersecting your route down below.

The road you are on now climbs slightly before beginning a gradual descent toward Transfer Trail with excellent views south. Back at Transfer Trail, turn right heading back to the saddle and back down the road. Either jump off onto the single-track or stay on the road until Traver Trail Road for the walk back to Hwy. 6&24. Either retrace your steps through the neighborhood or stay on the highway to the Colorado River pedestrian crossing into town.

With a car: Drive up Traver Trail Road and park at the pull-out mentioned. For no extra-credit whatsoever, drive up to the saddle and start the walk from there.

Walk #13: Windy Point

Downtown to Transfer Trail all the way to Windy Point and back to town.

Distance: 16.0 miles

Elevation Gain: 4500 feet

Difficulty: Moderate

Seasons: All but winter

Caveats: Watch for wildlife.

Description: Windy Point, in my estimation, is one of the finest viewpoints in the Glenwood area. A craggy bit of rock overlooking No Name Canyon provides a perfect, somewhat exposed, perch from which to survey the area. Looking north one sees the captivating rolling landscape of parkland dotted with forest, to the east the blocky ridge that divides No Name and Grizzly Creek. To the southeast and south, the Continental Divide, Elk Range and the Roaring Fork Valley.

Highlights: Views, Windy Point.

Amenities: None.

Directions: Follow Walk #12 to Transfer Trail, FS 602. Once on Transfer Trail follow this clear road as it climbs upward and onward to Windy Point. Most of the climbing takes place in the first six miles. The last two miles are less challenging.

Windy Point would be hard to miss. The road will suddenly burst out onto the open edge of No Name Canyon. A sign may warn of the number of fatalities that have occurred at this location by drivers who failed to turn. A flat rock outcropping with a somewhat garish red heart painted on its surface marks the best place to enjoy the view. Bring breakfast, lunch or dinner. Stay and savor the open air.

Return to Glenwood the way you came. If you meet any ATVers tell them where you've walked from and I guarantee they will be impressed!

Walk #14: Windy Point Bypass

Downtown to Transfer Trail to Windy Point, continuing on Transfer Trail to the Windy Point bypass route. Back to Transfer Trail and town.

Distance: 19.5 miles

Elevation Gain: 5200 feet

Difficulty: Difficult

Seasons: All but winter

Caveats: Snow north of Windy Point can last into early summer.

Description: This is a long walk and I don't just mean the distance. Something about this route always ends up making it feel longer than it is. Regardless, the ridge that the bypass follows has outstanding views south and Windy Point is superlative. The bypass also sees less traffic than Transfer Trail so if you do find yourself out in the middle of ATV season, the bypass can provide some peace that you might not find on the main road.

Highlights: Windy Point, the ridgeline the bypass follows.

Amenities: None.

Directions: Follow Walk #13 to Windy Point. From Windy Point continue on the road as it heads onto the north side of the ridge into dark forest. Snow will linger on this stretch into June and even early July.

Continue through cool dark forest for almost two miles to a meadow opening. Notice two yellow posts and a 4WD track on the left (south) entering into forest. Turn left onto this track and follow it for three miles as it winds up through forest onto the ridge where views open to the south before dropping into burnt forest to rejoin the Transfer Trail.

Back at Transfer Trail take a right and continue descending back to town the way that you came.

Alternatively, follow Walk #13 toward Windy Point. Two miles before Windy Point, notice a signed "Windy Point Bypass" ATV track on the left. Turn here and follow the bypass up onto the ridge crest. Wind through forest and drop briefly down to Transfer Trail. Turn right (east) to Windy Point and back to town.

Walk #15: Mitchell Creek

Downtown to Transfer Trail and Windy Point continuing on to Mitchell Creek for unforgettable descent to the Fish Hatchery and into Glenwood.

Distance: 20.0 miles

Difficulty: Expert

Elevation Gain: 5100 feet

Seasons: Spring and Fall

Caveats: The Mitchell Creek Trail has not received much TLC in recent years. As a result it is crisscrossed with fallen trees and profoundly overgrown with vegetation that bites (nettles and thorny brush). The trail is easy to lose and the trail surface requires a fair amount of attention as it is perfect ankle-breaking material. This trail requires stamina and a head for staying calm in the face of adversity. Long sleeves and pants are a must. In the peak of summer when vegetation is at its fullest I would leave it alone. A topographical map may help with navigation on Mitchell Creek

Description: As I write this I am not even sure that I should be including Mitchell Creek in this guide. However, the trail is on all the local trail maps and so it seems that it does deserve mention. It is also a trail that has gotten under my skin. Travelling its course can be a brutal, masochistic exercise but it is also joyous as the trail receives essentially no traffic and is therefore quite wild. Something about the way the light filters through the burnt trees and the sound of the creek keeps drawing me back. The reason I have described this walk as a loop beginning on the Transfer Trail and ending with Mitchell Creek is because I think it is ultimately easier to descend along the Creek than it is to navigate up. However, this is a loop that could be walked in either direction. Or, most sensibly drive to the fish hatchery (the nearest parking to the beginning of the trail), park, wander up towards Mitchell Creek and turn back to the safety and comfort of civilization if it begins to seem too much. I have provided directions from the fish hatchery to the beginning of the Mitchell Creek Trail. Just giving this trail a try deserves major kudos.

Highlights: Windy Point, Mitchell Creek

Amenities: Mitchell Creek is a healthy looking creek and filtered water from it would be fine. Fish Hatchery Visitor Center has water and bathroom

Directions: Follow Walk #14 to the Windy Point bypass. Instead of taking the bypass continue on Transfer Trail a quarter of a mile farther to a little opening over a vale on the left (south) that may or may not be signed with a "no 4WD" carsonite post. A track cuts down through the parkland towards a grove of aspen. Continue down along the western edge of the shallow drainage to a sizable cattle pond, stopping to check out the variety of footprints in the soft mud.

From the pond look due south. The track, mere single-track now, continues. A colored ribbon tied to a fir tree may mark the trail. Otherwise, simply follow the still shallow drainage on its western side (right bank). Carvings of initials and dates on a prominent old aspen tree let one know that one is on course. In this higher, more alpine setting travel is easy. Mitchell Creek is a trickle through here and often flows underground.

The vegetation begins to thicken but does not present too much of a problem until the creek begins to bend toward the south/southwest, about two and a half miles from where one began the descent into Mitchell Creek. Stay on the north side of the creek (the same side you've been on) following elk paths or whatever other routes make for the easiest going through waist high shrubbery. Just below where a drainage joins Mitchell Creek from the east/northeast (sometimes dry) the trail should pick up again.

From here, I cannot easily describe the route. The next two miles may begin to seem like the longest you have walked in your life. Vegetation is thick and obstructs visibility. The trail does cross the creek twice. One of these crossings actually has a fine log bridge with little hatchet steps cut into it. Finding these crossings is easier said than done. At times the creek makes use of the trail, so pay close attention when it is time to exit the creek onto trail.

Either way, if travels seems even harder than it should, there is a good chance that you are off-route. Keep mentally noting when you are on actual trail and back track when necessary. Staying on the real trail, as vague and indiscernible as it may be will still be easier than engaging in a total bushwhack.

After two miles the trail opens up and turns into a road/driveway. A happy sight indeed. Continue on the rough road as it quickly turns into progressively better road and arrives at the fish hatchery. From here, follow Walk #4 into town or to the bus stop at Mel-Ray and Hwy. 6&24.

Mitchell Creek from the Fish Hatchery: Follow Walk #4 or drive to the fish hatchery's visitor parking area. From the hatchery continue up the road as it becomes increasingly narrow and rougher. A sign marks that the road is not for thru-traffic and notes that there are mountain lions in the area. Walk past several residences to the road end. On the left (west) side of the drainage, at the northern grassy edge of the road-end, there is a metal forest service sign for Mitchell Creek Trail #1845. Good luck!

No Name (North)

While Transfer Trail switchbacks up exposed hillside to reach the Flat Tops, the No Name trail follows No Name Creek as it descends with icy cold delicious water from the Flat Tops. The walk up No Name, especially the first three miles from the trailhead to a crossing of the creek on a bridge, is quite delightful. The trail is well-used and well-maintained. It parallels the creek quite closely which provides natural air-conditioning on a hot summer day and plenty of water for the thirsty canine walking companion. The variety of vegetation as the trail climbs is striking and much of it edible: thimbleberries, serviceberries, choke cherries and raspberries all grow along the trail. In some of the damp woody sections, nettles grow.

Beyond the bridge crossing, the trail sees far less use and becomes a bit more challenging with overgrowth and poor tread in places. However, the scenery also becomes more striking as the trail continues climbing above the Creek. The trail weaves in and out of aspen groves and waterfalls farther ahead on the trail come into view. Two miles from the first creek crossing one comes to a sad sight: a plaque with a mention of Jess Weaver and his drowning at this crossing some years ago. A bridge was built in his memory and for the safety of others, but disappointingly the bridge has been allowed to go to ruin. Situated at the bottom of a narrow gorge water rushes in torrents during the height of run-off and has successfully pushed the bridge from its moorings and battered it into compromised submission. The bridge, broken in two, provides little comfort in a crossing. I would not recommend trying to cross before July, and in a big snow year even this may be too early. Shortly after this less than ideal crossing, one arrives at yet another bridge and the sight of a fine waterfall.

From this crossing, the trail continues up to a knoll that sits between No Name and its eastern fork, East No Name Creek. From here one has a choice of two trails. The more prominent trail bends northwest and continues along No Name Creek. The other trail travels along East No Name Creek.

No Name is at its best during the spring, summer and fall. During the winter this trail does not see a lot of use and for good reason: the steep slopes can be quite avalanche prone. If in need of a snowshoe trip, Lookout Mountain and Transfer Trail are better bets.

Walk #16: Jess Weaver Trail

Downtown to the Glenwood Canyon Trail to the tiny non-commercial settlement of No Name and the Jess Weaver trailhead, up No Name Creek and then back to town.

Distance: 6.0 – 18.0+ miles

Elevation Gain: 700 – 3800 feet

Difficulty: Moderate

Seasons: All but winter

Caveats: The crossing of No Name on the Jess Weaver bridge should not be taken lightly. In anything but the lowest of water levels this ford is a potential death sentence.

Description: The Jess Weaver Trail is a favorite. The great majority of walkers drive to the trailhead and enjoy a three-mile walk to the first crossing of the creek before turning around back to the trailhead for a comfortable six mile walk. With a little gumption though, one can easily enjoy a walk from Glenwood to the Jess Weaver trailhead. The Glenwood Canyon Trail is a great bicycle path and even this short walk along it gives a great taste of what it would be like journey its length. No Name is a pleasant little community sandwiched between steep hills and the river. If one makes only the trailhead the perfectly worthy destination, it is a seven mile round-trip walk from Glenwood. Adding the six mile round-trip to the first crossing makes for a thirteen mile adventure. Continuing farther along the Jess Weaver trail adds even more miles. For a complete taste of the Jess Weaver Trail, continue just past the third bridge to the knoll between No Name and East No Name Creeks. Roundtrip from downtown, this is a full eighteen miles with 3800 feet of gain.

Walk! Glenwood Springs Town and Hills

Highlights: Horseshoe Bend, No Name Creek and water flume, bridges over the creek.

Amenities: Interstate rest area on the Colorado River at No Name exit. No Name water is great with a filter.

Directions: From 8th Street and the west side of Grand Avenue in downtown Glenwood follow the pedestrian mall to 7th Street. Cross 7th to stairs just ahead and on the right that lead to a pedestrian bridge across the Colorado River. Pass the pool, and mini-golf course and turn right (east), passing in front of the Hotel Colorado. Continue past the Hot Springs Lodge, the Glenwood Arts Center and the Yampah Vapor Caves to the entrance of the Glenwood Canyon bicycle path and an informational sign about big horn sheep which are often seen in the canyon. Closely parallel the interstate for almost one mile to an overhead crossing which leads into Horseshoe Bend. This amphitheater of rock is striking and without I-70 running through it, the trail begins to feel like something of a getaway.

The bicycle path soon exits Horseshoe Bend onto paved street. Follow this as it approaches the interchange at I-70. Turn left (north), cross over the interstate and continue north past several residences to the end of the road and the clearly signed Jess Weaver trailhead (3.5 miles from Glenwood). Follow the gated road which climbs steeply initially to waterworks and an aqueduct on No Name creek. Notice remnants of old water flume high above on the west side of the creek. The route becomes single-track at this point, travelling on the left (west) bank of the creek.

Follow the trail as it ascends along the drainage. Mile posts, some of them quite tattered, help count the miles. Just past milepost three, the trail turns toward the creek and onto a bridge. This is a great place to turn around, six and a half miles from Glenwood.

From here the trail continues to a switchback and then again heads north paralleling, but now considerably farther above, the creek. Through aspen groves and across rock fall the trail continues, in places becoming quite brushy and overgrown (watch for nettles!). After two miles, and now quite close to the creek, the dilapidated Jess Weaver Bridge comes into sight.

Carefully assess water levels and determine whether or not you are putting your life at risk if you cross. If you cannot see an easy route across the creek, ***DO NOT CROSS***.

If water levels are safely low, cross the creek and scramble up the rocky trail to better tread just ahead. Look for raspberries growing along here. The trail switchbacks and continues north to yet another crossing of No Name Creek, this time on a bridge that is subject to less wear and tear and is withstanding the test of time. Continue on trail through aspen and some brush to a knoll between No Name and East No Name Creeks just above the spot where No Name Creek bends to the west. At this point, you are six miles from the trailhead, and nine miles from downtown Glenwood. From here the trail continues and the East No Name Trail has its southern terminus. Details of these routes can be found in Walk #18 and Walk #19.

With a car: From Glenwood hop on eastbound I-70 to the next exit, No Name. From the exit travel north on a short, dead-ending stretch of county road. The road ends at the trailhead.

Walk #17: No Name/Grizzly Creeks

Downtown to No Name and the Jess Weaver Trail, east to the saddle between No Name and Grizzly Creeks, down to Grizzly Creek and back to town on the Glenwood Canyon Trail.

Distance: 11.0 – 17.0 miles

Elevation Gain: 3900 feet

Difficulty: Difficult

Seasons: Summer and Fall

Caveats: There is not a bridge across Grizzly Creek. The creek must be forded. Do not attempt this crossing in anything but the lowest of water. Also keep an eye out for wildlife, especially bear, between No Name and Grizzly Creeks.

Description: This is a classic walk over a low-point in the ridge that separates No Name from Grizzly Creek. The saddle between the two is clearly visible from both Red and Lookout Mountains. The trails that parallel both creeks are in great shape, while the stretch connecting the two is always something of an adventure requiring a bit of fortitude. I would recommend long sleeves and pants. Grizzly Creek does not have a bridge over its crossing. For this reason, summer and fall are the only seasons that permit this walk. In the spring the run-off through Grizzly Creek is far too great to allow for a safe crossing. In fact, it would likely be a quick and deadly trip down to the Colorado. Should water be high, hiking from No Name only as far as the saddle is a worthy effort in itself.

Highlights: Lofty saddle between No Name and Grizzly Creeks, Grizzly Creek Trail, Glenwood Canyon Trail.

Amenities: Interstate rest areas at both No Name and Grizzly Creek exits.

Directions: Follow directions for Walk #16 to the Jess Weaver trailhead and along No Name to the first creek crossing, just over three miles up the trail. Cross the bridge and continue on a switchback. Look for a small cairn in the grass next to the trail on the right hand side. While the main trail continues north, a somewhat less distinct trail forks south/southeast.

This is your trail. Follow it through scrubby shrubbery as it switchbacks higher into aspen groves. Near the saddle, the elk seem to do a great job maintaining the trail and the path is well worn and fairly easy to follow. The saddle is obvious and, while you will not be able to see Grizzly Creek below, you will be looking into its canyon. Standing at the saddle, look down into Grizzly and hopefully spot the faint path cutting through the sturdy vegetation. Carefully begin working your way down, adhering to the trail as strictly as possible. The route down is considerably steeper and more direct than the trail you came up. As you near the creek you will see a sizable aqueduct that cuts through the ridge you just came over, bringing water to Glenwood. The trail arrives on the western bank of the creek in a pile of deadwood and vegetation. A cairn on the other side usually marks the route up to the Grizzly Creek trail. Carefully assess water levels and whether crossing is worth your life.

Assuming a safe crossing, the Grizzly Creek Trail can be found on the eastern bank, just above the creek. It is well-used and begins an easy, relaxed descent towards I-70 and the Colorado River. After almost three and a half miles one reaches the Grizzly Creek trailhead (just north of I-70). Pass under the interstate and onto the Glenwood Canyon Trail. Turn right (west) and stay on the paved path back to No Name and into Glenwood.

Note: I do not recommend this loop in reverse, starting on Grizzly Creek. The vegetation on the slope above Grizzly Creek up to the saddle grows with a downward orientation. I find it much easier to flow down the hill with it. Going up this slope feels like more of a fight and I often feel as if the plants are trying to push me back down.

With a car: Park at either the Jess Weaver trailhead, the No Name rest area or the Grizzly Creek rest area. Parking at one of these areas takes six miles off the total distance, reducing the walk to approximately 11.0 miles.

Walk #18: Windy Point via No Name

Downtown to Jess Weaver trail along the length of No Name to Transfer Trail, Windy Point and back to Glenwood.

Distance: 23.0 miles

Elevation Gain: 5400 feet

Difficulty: Difficult

Seasons: Spring, Summer, Fall

Caveats: Watch for Wildlife. Late snow above 10,000 ft. can make for slow going in the spring time. The descent from Windy Point can be dry and hot in summer. Carrying a topographical map is recommended.

Description: This walk is one of my personal favorites. I love the prolonged yet comfortable ascent along No Name creek. I never tire of seeing how the landscape and vegetation changes with the elevation. From where the Jess Weaver Trail bends to the west, I find myself admiring the creek which through here reminds me of streams in Appalachia, blocky flat rocks form the walls and floor of the creek bed. The creek becomes wide and flat as the trail begins to level out. Beavers have made their homes here and their architectural masterpieces in the form of dams and pools are fun to observe. Soon after passing a disintegrating old hunting cabin the single-track turns to jeep track. Continue climbing gradually to an intersection with the Transfer Trail. Once on the Transfer Trail the cruising is easy although there is still almost 500 feet of gain ahead. The Transfer Trail turns east, topping out at 10,500 feet. From here it is all downhill and from Windy Point the descent is fun and fast.

Highlights: No Name Creek, Windy Point.

Amenities: Water for filtering in creeks. No water once on Transfer Trail.

Directions: Follow Walk #16 along the Jess Weaver Trail to the knoll between No Name and East No Name Creeks. Here the trail may be a little faint as it bends west/northwest above No Name Creek following the creek as it also bends toward the west. The trail begins to climb much more gradually than it has been and provides a peaceful stroll through aspen, fir, and meadowland.

The trail stays clearly on the north side of the creek. Follow it as it passes beaver ponds, an old cabin, and turns into jeep track. From the cabin and the beginning of the jeep track continue not even a mile to the well-used Transfer Trail. Turn left (south) onto the road and soon wade or use stepping stones across No Name. Stay on the road as it ascends gradually. Look for elk, bear and other wildlife.

Signed roads will point the way to Yellow and Haypress Lakes. Stay on Transfer Trail (FS602). Follow Transfer Trail as it makes a clear bend to the east and enters cooler, darker forest. Continuing east/southeast for two miles from the bend brings one to the magnificent views of Windy Point. From here stay on the road for a fast downhill to Glenwood! See Walk #12 for details on the route back to Glenwood if at all uncertain.

Note: This loop works well in either direction. If it is a really hot summer day I may head up the dry, exposed slopes of the Transfer Trail toward Windy Point early in the morning and then enjoy a cooler walk down No Name in the heat of the day. To walk it in this direction, follow Walk #13 up to Windy Point and then continue on FS 602 to No Name Creek and the lesser used 4WD track which turns into the Jess Weaver Trail.

With a car: Since this walk ends in Glenwood instead of returning to No Name, a shuttle would be necessary.

Walk! Glenwood Springs Town and Hills

Leave one car at the No Name trailhead and another at the pull-out on Traver Trail Road at the junction with Transfer Trail. Shuttling cars would take approximately four miles off the total distance. See Walk #12 for more information.

Walk #19: East No Name

Downtown to No Name and the Jess Weaver Trail to East No Name Creek to Bowen Lake and back along No Name Creek.

Distance: 18.5 – 24.5 miles

Elevation Gain: 5700 feet

Difficulty: Expert

Seasons: Summer, Fall

Caveats: The East No Name Trail is quite vague from start to finish. A topographical map is essential. Watch for wildlife.

Description: The East No Name Trail is a neglected treasure in my opinion. The trail is a relatively short two miles, connecting the No Name Trail with a forest service road, although keep in mind that one must first walk at least six miles to reach this trail. The trail provides direct access up to the Flat Tops and is a pleasing walking experience. The East No Name Trail wraps around a somewhat wet hillside before dropping slightly to a crossing of East No Name Creek. From there it climbs a little above and away from the creek, paralleling the creek on its east side. A little set of rock stairs and a clear, short switchback let one know that one is on route. The trail continues through increasingly open forest to a junction with a forest service road. This walk would also lend itself well to an overnight backpacking trip.

Highlights: East No Name Trail, Bowen Lake, No Name Creek

Amenities: Plenty of water for filtering in No Name and East No Name Creeks.

Directions: Follow Walk #16 on the Jess Weaver Trail until reaching the knoll that sits between No Name and

East No Name Creeks. As you walk the last steps onto this knoll through aspen you will notice milepost #6 on your left. A few steps beyond look to your right for anything trail-like and a sizable aspen which has ENN and an arrow carved into its trunk at eye level. This aspen tree points in the right direction and is the most tangible, permanent marker for the start of the trail. The trail climbs a little but mostly contours toward the east across somewhat marshy, vegetated slopes. At times the trail is astonishingly clear, at other times frustratingly vague. Watch for bear through here hiding in the growth. After contouring north/northeast the trail begins to bend northward and drops to a crossing of East No Name Creek. Push through vegetation on the other side to come onto more open gentle slopes.

Stay on the east side of the creek, following the trail as closely as possible as it continues to climb through a little swithchback. The trail straightens its course and proceeds until intersecting a dirt forest service road one mile after the creek crossing. Note where you arrive at the road if you plan to descend by this route as there are not any trail markers.

This is also a fine place to turn around. You are now ten miles from downtown Glenwood. The route I suggest from here is just one of many possible loops that one can make to sightsee the southern edge of the Flat Tops.

Turn left (north/northwest) onto the forest service road and follow it to its end at another forest service road at Bowen Lake, which sits below the southern edge of rocky Baxter Peak (11185 ft.) and the remains of a primitive cabin. Turn left (west/southwest) onto this road and continue until the road ends at the larger and better used Transfer Trail (FS 602). Turn left (south) on Transfer Trail and after just barely half a mile look for a minor track on your left (south/southeast). This rougher 4WD track parallels No Name Creek on its north side.

The track traverses open meadow, passes a series of beaver ponds and dams and a cabin that has seen better days. Along the way you may notice mileposts seven and eight – yes, you are back on the Jess Weaver Trail. The road narrows to single track near an old cabin and begins to close in on No Name Creek with its rock-lined little gorge and creek bed. When the creek begins to cascade into waterfalls, the trail bends toward the little knoll between No Name and East No Name Creeks where you began this loop.

Continue on the Jess Weaver Trail back to the trailhead and back to Glenwood.

With a car: Park at the No Name trailhead to shave six miles off the total trip.

Walk #20: Flat Tops Wilderness

Downtown Glenwood to Jess Weaver Trail and onto the East No Name Trail, continuing along East No Name Creek to a junction with a forest service road near a neatly kept cabin (private). North on old jeep/pack trail to Palmer Lake. Head northwest, onto the Transfer Trail to White Owl Lake and Coffee Pot Road. Take Coffee Pot Road to the east side of Heart Lake and a jeep road heading north along Buck Creek past Triangle Mountain to Indian Camp Pass and the boundary of the Flat Tops Wilderness.

Distance: 27.0 miles *one-way*

Elevation Gain: 6050 feet

Difficulty: Expert

Seasons: All but winter

Caveats: Topographical maps are a must. Plan for all weather, even in the summer. The Flat Tops can and do see snow all months of the year. Watch for wildlife.

Description: Let me be the first to admit that there is something a little insane about walking from Glenwood to the edge of the Flat Tops Wilderness. I have done this walk several times and the amusement factor is huge and for that reason I want to share it. I am not sure if I end up smiling just because it is a little unusual to walk somewhere that most people drive to or whether it is because there is a fair amount of really great scenery between here and there. Either way, having walked several routes to the Flat Tops I can say that this is the most direct route and easiest. Turn this into a multi-day backpacking trip by looping through the Wilderness (be sure to bring maps).

Highlights: No Name and East No Name Creeks, Heart Lake, Indian Camp Pass, Flat Tops Wilderness.

Amenities: Filterable water on route.

Directions: Follow Walk #19 to where the East No Name Trail intersects a forest service road. From the junction of the East No Name Trail and the forest service road, pull out the topographical map and note East No Name Creek continuing to the north. Follow the drainage on it west side (cross-country) past a beautiful little pond/lake (dry spot in dry years). The travel is easy and game trails make it even easier. One mile from the first road crossing you will see a cabin (private) on the left (west) and arrive at another forest service road.

Cross the road and continue north along the west side of the East No Name drainage. Colored flags, faint tire marks, and equestrian hoof marks are all evidence of being on route. The trail is mostly single track and for the most part easy to discern. Pass a couple of ponds and walk through what is sometimes a damp water-sodden terrain to a bit of forest with lots of logging evidence to Palmer Lake. Skirt the lake on its west side to its inlet (if Palmer Lake is a clock face, 9 o'clock is your time) and look for the trail as it continues toward the west/northwest. The single track soon turns to old road bed and descends out of forest into a lowland opening and easily crosses South Grizzly Creek. Continue on the road to its intersection with ample, well-used Transfer Trail. Turn northward (right) onto the road and follow it past Duck Lake, Grizzly Lake and to within sight of White Owl Lake.

From the overlook above White Owl Lake, you have a choice to either stay on the road as it skirts to the east side of the lake and arrives at Coffee Pot Road or to do a little shortcut by travelling cross-country staying above the lake, contouring around on its west side and then picking up a faint road which also leads to Coffee Pot Road. Standing above White Owl Lake it is possible to see both options clearly below and make an educated decision as to the best route for you.

Now on well-used and well-maintained but unpaved Coffee Pot Road turn left (northwest) toward Heart Lake. Just before the lake, the road forks with Coffee Pot Road heading for camping at the southern end of the lake. Take the right fork, off of Coffee Pot Road to stay on the east side of the lake, continuing north.

Stay on this road past the lake as it bends toward the northeast. Keep an eye on the road you are on and the map, as there is something of a tangle of 4WD track in this area. Use Buck Creek as your guide and stay on obvious road on its west side. The road crosses to the east side of Buck Creek just before Triangle Mountain. Continue on the road for a little over one more mile before gradually descending to Indian Camp Pass with a sign and trail register for the Flat Tops Wilderness. Nice work!

With a car: Drive on Coffee Pot Road (from Glenwood take I-70 east to the Dotsero Exit and Coffee Pot Road) to the Flat Tops Wilderness. Alternatively, walk from Glenwood to the wilderness area and arrange for car pick-up.

To Carbondale (South)

While many bicyclists ride between Glenwood and Carbondale on the Rio Grande Trail, I do not think that many walkers consider travelling on foot between the two towns. For a unique walking experience I would recommend the trip. There are two different routes that I choose between when I am thinking of making my way to Carbondale on foot. Both of these routes are quite worthy in their own right and not at all alike. The best part about making the walk is that one does not need to feel stranded upon reaching Carbondale or envision a long march back. The public bus serves downtown Carbondale on Main Street, across from the post office, with regular service back to Glenwood. Carbondale has some great restaurants and cafes and fun shopping so make a day of it!

Walk #22: Rio Grande Bicycle Path

Downtown Glenwood to Carbondale along the paved Rio Grande rail-trail.

Distance: 13.0 miles

Elevation Gain: 300 feet

Difficulty: Moderate

Seasons: All year

Caveats: In the depth of winter the trail may have snow in places.

Description: Follow the Rio Grande Trail from downtown Glenwood to downtown Carbondale.

Highlights: The Rio Grande Trail (converted railroad right-of-way), downtown Carbondale.

Amenities: Six miles into the walk is the Thunder River Market convenience store on Hwy. 82. There is also a bus stop at this intersection should one want to either rewind to Glenwood or fast forward to Carbondale. Well-maintained, permanent outhouse just prior to Aspen Glen subdivision, three miles before Carbondale.

Directions: From 8th and Grand Avenue in downtown Glenwood follow Grand south to 11th Street. Turn right (west) past the 7-11 and then turn left (north) on Colorado. Proceed to what is called the 12th Street cut. There is not a street, but a path alongside a small gully that may be signed as "River Trail". Turn right on this well-used path and follow it two blocks until it intersects the obvious Rio Grande Trail. Turn left onto the Trail. This is your path to Carbondale!

The Rio Grande parallels Hwy. 82 from a short distance for the majority of the miles to Carbondale.

Alternate start: For purists who want to follow the Rio Grande Trail from the very beginning, follow directions from Walk #1 to Two Rivers Park. The hefty bridge across the Colorado marks the beginning of the rail-trail. Once arriving at the bridge and taking photos, turn eyes and body south for the walk to Carbondale.

With a car: Park in downtown if planning to catch the bus back, otherwise park at Two Rivers Park or one of the automobile access points along the Rio Grande.

Walk! Glenwood Springs Town and Hills

Walk #23: Dry Park

Downtown Glenwood to Cardiff Glen and Four-Mile Road (CR 117), up Four-Mile to Dry Park Road (CR 125) across the private Crystal River Ranch property to Thompson Creek Road (CR 108) into Carbondale

Distance: 14.0 miles

Elevation Gain: 2000 feet

Difficulty: Difficult

Seasons: Spring, Summer, Fall

Description: This is a superlative walk although considerably more demanding than taking the Rio Grande to Carbondale. The effort required is greater but so are the rewards. The route begins easily enough to Cardiff. From there, one begins to climb steadily along Four-Mile Road to Dry Park Road. The upward trend continues until one is well above the valley floor enjoying territorial views. Dry Park Road levels out before arriving at Thompson Creek Road CR 108 where a steady descent brings one to a crossing of the Crystal River and soon after to the center of Carbondale.

Highlights: Cardiff Glen, Four-Mile Road, Dry Park Road and Crystal River Ranch, downtown Carbondale.

Amenities: Market and gas station in Cardiff Glen near entrance to Four-Mile Road, nothing between Cardiff and Carbondale.

Directions: Follow Walk #3 to the Atkinson Trail and the riverside picnic area. From here, instead of taking a side trail into the neighborhood, stay on the dominant trail travelling away from the river. Follow this trail until it ends at Midland Avenue near the market and gas station. Turn left, pass the market, cross Mt. Sopris Drive, stay on path for a short distance until signs for Sunlight Ski Area and Four Mile Road (CR117) appear. Turn right (west) onto Four Mile Road and begin to climb steadily past a fire station and newer developments. Be mindful of traffic.

Dry Park Road will be on the left (south), after approximately two miles. It is well signed. Turn left and follow Dry Park Road as it climbs steadily through the Crystal River Ranch property. Stay on the road as the property to either side is private. Thanks to the ranch, views are lofty and unobstructed by development. Traffic tends to be light. As the road climbs, the views become better and better. Mt. Sopris looms ahead and in the springtime bluebirds are abundant.

Dry Park Road ends at Thompson Creek Road. Turn left, downhill, and follow this road, also lightly travelled, to its crossing of the Crystal River near the Colorado Rocky Mountain School. Now on the north side of the river, parallel it and the road on paved path soon arriving at the commercial center of Carbondale at Highway 133 and Main Street. Continue straight onto Main Street as it makes a little jog soon arriving in downtown Carbondale.

With a car: Park in downtown Glenwood.

Appendix 1: Walks by Difficulty

Rating walks based on their difficulty is extremely subjective. For that reason I have listed all of the walks here with the rating I have given and the reason, so that you can use your own judgment as to whether the walk would be a good fit or not. All of the walks in the guide are labeled Easy, Moderate, Difficult or Expert. Easy walks are those that utilize almost exclusively paved, level surfaces. Moderate walks may be on mixed surfaces and very likely involve elevation gain. Navigation should not present a challenge. Difficult walks follow longer, steeper and more poorly surfaced trail. In places the route may be vague and require extra attention. The walks labeled as expert require a great deal of fortitude as they are much more challenging in terms of length, walking surface, and navigation.

Easy Walks:

#1 – Two Rivers - Paved surfaces, level

#2 – 27th Street - Paved surfaces, level

#3 – Cardiff Glen - Good surfaces, level

#6 – Wulfsohn Open Space - Good surfaces, little elevation gain

Moderate Walks:

#4 – West Glenwood: Longer route with some elevation gain on good surfaces

#5 – Jeanne Golay Trail: Steady climb on natural surfaces

#7 – Doc Holliday: Steady climb on natural surfaces

#8 – Scout Trail: Steady climb on natural surfaces

#11 – Red Canyon: Long, primarily natural surfaces; lengthy descent helps miles fly

#12 – Transfer Trail: Steady climb on natural surfaces

#13 – Windy Point: Steady climb on natural surfaces

#16 – Jess Weaver Trail: Steady climb on natural surfaces

#21 – Rio Grande: Long but with paved surfaces and relatively level

Difficult Walks:

#9 – Lookout Mountain Proper: Longer route on natural surfaces with some brushy, overgrown trail

#10 – Bear Creek: Lengthy route, steady climb, natural surfaces

#14 – Windy Point Bypass: Lengthy loop on natural surfaces

#17 – No Name/Grizzly Creeks: Steady climb on natural surfaces, 1½ miles on easy-to-lose brushy overgrown trail

#18 – Windy Point via No Name: Steady climb on natural surfaces, some sections on rough trail

#23 – Dry Park: Lengthy route, steady climb, some natural surfaces

Expert Walks:

#15 – Mitchell Creek: Overgrown trail with poor tread and potential for navigational problems

#19 – East No Name: Steady climb on natural surfaces, neglected stretch of trail requires extra attention

#20 – Flat Tops Wilderness: Lengthy route with steady climb, some route-finding required with potential for navigational problems

Reading List

These are just a few of my favorite reads that are about walking or have walking as a central theme. The books range in time and place, fiction and non-fiction. All of these books provide great food for thought as you find yourself sampling walks around Glenwood.

Craig Childs, *Soul of Nowhere*, 2002. Explorations on foot of harsh landscapes and prehistory in the Southwest United States. Natural History.

Joshua Ferris, *The Unnamed*, 2010. Life is fine until the protagonist starts to walk. A novel about the mind and body in the 21st century. Fiction, novel.

John Francis, *Planetwalker*, 2008. A completely original account of finding oneself through walking and silence. Environment, personal growth.

Linda Hunt, *Bold Spirit: Helga Estby's Forgotten Walk across Victorian America*, 2005. A mother and daughter walk from Washington State to New York. History.

Stephen King, *The Long Walk*, 1979. Death march contest in a totalitarian US. Horror, fiction, novel.

John Lewis, *Walking with the Wind: A Memoir of the Movement*, 1998. A legendary civil-rights leader (and still congressman) eloquently captures the key role of walking in community and social change. Autobiography.

Richard Louv, *Last Child in the Woods: Saving Our Children from Nature-Deficit Disorder*, 2005. Nuanced discussion of nature's role in a digital era. Psychology and Nature, Landscape Design.

Geoff Nicholson, *The Lost Art of Walking: the History, Science, Philosophy, and Literature of Pedestrianism*, 2008. Unabashed stream-of-conscious observations on walking highlight the interplay between internal dialogues and external landscapes during walking. Walking History.

Peace Pilgrim: Her Life and Work in Her Own Words, 1983. Walking with political and spiritual purpose. Spirituality, Grassroots Political Action.

Slavomir Rawicz, *The Long Walk,* 1997. The ultimate Siberian Gulag escape story. Fiction/History.

Rebecca Solnit, *Wanderlust: A History of Walking,* 2000. An overview of walking and the human experience. Walking History.

Henry David Thoreau, *Essays: Walking, A Winter Walk,* Lewis Hyde, ed, 2002. Classics. History, Environment.

Glenwood Springs History

Jim Nelson, *Glenwood Springs: the History of a Rocky Mountain Resort,* 1999.

Acknowledgements

Without Glenwood Springs this little book would not exist so I first must thank the City of Glenwood Springs for constantly considering pedestrian well-being. From the landscaping and art surrounding walkways to the city crews diligently keeping paths plowed on the snowiest days, Glenwood does a great job taking care of its walkers.

Gary Grillo of the Glenwood Springs Hostel, now retired, pointed me toward the hills and their paths soon after I arrived in Glenwood. More often than not, far from town on a little used trail I'd suddenly sense someone at find Gary out on his own romping around the hills. He'd be the only soul I'd see out all day. He gave me some good comments after seeing a final draft of this guide.

My walking partner Colleen Rutledge provided the inspiration to write down these walks and was also essential in helping edit and lending polish with her cracker-jack language skills. I am indebted. She also contributed photos for which I am grateful.

Having walked these trails many years more than I and having spent a lifetime looking at guidebooks of all kinds, Tony Angelis offered invaluable comment and critique. A stickler for detail, the final product is superior for Tony's assistance.

I am grateful to Carol of Glenwood's independent bookstore, The Book Train, who offered me encouragement and guidance investigating publishing options.

My friend Joe Norman contributed photos and editing help, and deserves a special thanks for always believing in me.

Photos by Chapter

All photos by author unless otherwise noted.

Cover: Glenwood Springs from Red Mountain.

In Town: Plaque at 6th and Grand Avenue.

Walk #1: Storm King Memorial in Two Rivers Park.

Walk #2: Glenwood Sidewalk in Winter.

Red Mountain: Mt. Sopris from Red Mountain, by Joe Norman

Walk #5: Jeanne Golay Trail sign.

Walk #7: Doc Holiday, Pioneer Cemetery, by Joe Norman.

Walk #9: Descending Doc Holiday's Cemetery Gulch trail in winter.

Walk #11: Bear print on Lookout Mountain Road near radio towers.

No Name: Looking down No Name from the old Jess Weaver Bridge.

Walk #16: No Name at high water; Jess Weaver plaque near bridge remains.

Walk #19: No Name drainage from No Name/Grizzly/Creek saddle.

To Carbondale: Downtown Carbondale banners.

Walk #22: Beginning of the Rio Grande trail in Two Rivers Park.

Walk #23: View from Dry Park Road.

About the Author

My family moved from an urban setting in one state to the countryside of another during the summer I was 13. Without a car and not knowing anyone, I started wandering down country roads. A few miles soon turned into walks of 12–25 miles.

It wasn't until age 25 that I began to wonder what it would be like to walk every day, day after day, which kicked off more than a decade of distance walking. In 2000, with my dear friend Joe Norman, I walked the Oregon Coast Trail. I spent the summers of 2001, 2002, and 2003 on the Pacific Crest Trail, ultimately walking much of the trail twice. In 2004 I was on the Arizona Trail with hiking partner Brian Frankle. With 2006 I took the walking overseas with a trip along England's longest national way-marked walking path: The Southwest Coast Path. Corsica's GR20, considered to be one of Europe's hardest, was 2007. In 2008 I tried out the Pyrenean High Route along the French-Spanish border from the Atlantic to the Mediterranean, as well as a jaunt in Morocco's Atlas Mountains. September 2009 found me walking converted rail-trail along British Columbia's Trans-Canada Trail. I decided to stay in my own backyard in 2011 and put in 1000 miles on the Continental Divide Trail, from New Mexico's boot heel to the heart of the Colorado Rockies. In the spring of 2012 I walked Britain End-to-End.

Exploring self-propelled transportation led me to hop on a bicycle with my dog in the front basket and ride from Glenwood Springs to Seattle in the fall of 2012, ultimately saying goodbye to Glenwood after a very good seven years.

To keep myself in walking shoes, bicycle tires, and my dog in quality kibbles, I currently work in Transportation Services at the University of Washington.

Made in the USA
Middletown, DE
17 June 2022